The Book of Clouds

Marc Zegans

Kite-string Press

The Book of Clouds by Marc Zegans

ISBN-13: 978-1-938349-60-7

Copyright © 2016 Marc Zegans

Library of Congress Cataloguing-in-publication Data

Marc Zegans 1961-

An offering of clouds in verse. A different cloud on which to sleep for each night of any month.

Kite-string Press in Association with Pelekinesis Publishing Group

    1.   Poetry 2. Dreams 3. Magical-realism 4. Love 5. Sleep

Layout and Book Design by Marc Zegans

The Book of Clouds by Marc Zegans

Copyright © 2016 Marc Zegans.

Second Kite-string Printing 2016

THE BOOK OF CLOUDS

For Meri

*May your only clouds in life
be those upon which you dream.*

i

"I would like you to make me a cloud tonight
a cloud hanging over the Pacific
high above the sunset, glowing with dusk.

I would like you to make me a cloud tonight,
tied by a long string to your rocking toe,
that travels all the way to Lexington
and greets me with an unfolding ladder.

I would like you to make me a cloud tonight
into which I climb sleepy and unbound
from the rumble and clatter of the day
foot after foot whisking the long ladder

as if I were free from all profane weight,
simply loose to rise in my bright spirit,
careless as the cloud on which I will sleep
while you sit on the beach in a small chair

your stringed toe rocking me on my cloud, gently."

"Would you like a cloud tonight?"

"I think so."

"What sort of cloud?"

"A simple cloud that you will pull
 with you as you walk the beach."

iii

"Your cloud tonight is white
fluffy and cumulous."

"Is cumulous a quality?"

"Absolutely."

iv

Tonight's cloud hangs low
heavy with night rain.

It will give its rain
to the earth, shortly—

when it meets your cheek.

v

You have a cloud of pink coral tonight
carried from Belize on gentle trade winds.
Its journey has made it softer than light
and it welcomes you as its beloved.

vi

Tonight's quiet cloud matches the moonlight.
It shines a happy white in the deep sky
as if it had a smile on its face,
but it needs no face to hold you with joy.

vii

As though dropping from a wall
you fall into tonight's spun grey cloud
softer than lambs wool, stronger than silk.

It stretches around your sides, cradling
your leap into dreamless sleep.

viii

Free and festive, rested now many days
you ask me for a cloud of vivid dreams
and I give you this cloud of radiant white
from which you can draw a million colors

strand upon strand
          on which to weave your dreams.

ix

This cloud imbibes layers of sunset
a parfait of violets, oranges,
lavenders, crimsons, maroons and blues

displaying them in wild bouquet
as you climb with slow steps into darkness
past the gatherings from this spry day.

x

"I want a very soft cloud please."
"Then you shall have it."

"And a very nice cloud…
And that you will rock it…

And a good cloud
that will keep me safe."

xi

The clouds this late summer evening,
arrayed above glistening waves,
mercury moonlight traveling
in streaks and beads along their curls,
have gathered seeking your favor.

Each wishes to be your one cloud
to be the one you will soon pick.
You eye each in turn with delight
examining its special gifts

its shapes, colors and qualities
and the songs it sings to your ear
until you find one so quiet
that to hear its gentle whisper
you must rise to its embrace.

xii

Your cloud tonight is thin
floating soft and gentle

three steps above your bed.

It travels while you sleep
so that you may enjoy
new vistas in your dreams.

xiii

Tonight's cloud, dollops and dollops of puff
is a candle in the night for putti
attracted by its vivacious fizz
and its occupant whom they greet with love.

"I did not know until now," you mention
"that renaissance painters were such realists.
They've captured these little fellows quite well
don't you think?" Their laughter thrills in your ears.

xiv

(c)loud
thunder

clap!

xv

The cloud zipped in a small bag
placed with care in your suitcase
has broad imagination.

When you need him in the sky
he will expand to the size
you ardently desire

taking on color and form
to match your sleeping wishes
so that you will wake with joy.

xvi

This cloud is quiet and a bit shy.
You will have to coax this cloud to come out.
It will want to know your evening's intent,
so that it can tell if it is the right cloud
or whether, perhaps, there has been a mix-up
and it is not your cloud or anyone's.
It would very much like to be your cloud,
but it would not like to be in error.

When you have assured this cloud that it is yours
it will swell with the golden light of kings
and unfold for you a great spiral stair
so warm that you will not have to wear socks.
When you have climbed to the top of this cloud
your ancient hurts will fall to earth as mist.

xvii

cloudmericloudcloud
cloudcloudcloudcloudcloud
clocloudcloudcloudud
cloudcloudcloud
cloudcloud
.
.
.
.
.
.

.

.

.

,
marc

xviii

Utterly and completely exhausted
you slide groggily into your cloud
its gathered spray enveloping you
cleansing the day from your weary eyes
bringing soothing light in your turn to sleep.

xix

From byzantine to aubergine
amethyst through mauve into orchid
eggplant entwined with english violet
the varied purples of your cloud
remove the robes of public office
leaving you only, ready for sleep.

xx

This cloud of yours, you have seen before
on a heated, distant summer night
hanging far over blacked Carrib sea
waiting for you to return
to your home and familiar bed.

It meets you now in the place you've made
inviting you to travel upward
and lie your head on pillow of wisp
above the willow in will-less rest.

xxi

Tonight's cloud has travelled far from the South
or perhaps it is the Earth that has travelled
while your cloud sits serene in what we call wind.

xxii

Your cloud glows Venetian Red
it has the scent of history
and the lushness of ripened fruit.
it will be here one night only
its color fading over time
like velvet worn bare to the warp

but tonight you will know its scent
wrap yourself in its luxury
and paint in Titian's poesie
your dreams, a flurry of soft strokes
blending one into the other
until all that remains is light.

xxiii

Imagine if the shifting stria
stretched and strewn cross tonight's western sky
were an atmospheric compression
unfolding over millions of years

and, in the timescale by which we see
eons only lingering moments.
Imagine that the cloud in foreground,
in sky remaining painterly blue,

the cloud that will take you into dream
travels fast as the sun's messenger
and that your journey on it tonight
will be a flash before the sunset

yet, an unfolding of great moment.

xxiv

Your cloud tonight is a delicious
confection of oranges and lemons
with enough cream to make a Pavlova.

It takes you to her house by Golders Hill.

XXV

This cloud floats over horses grazing
on the salt-breeze grass by Muir Beach.
It follows their return to stable
then travels by jet stream to meet you
the scents of eucalyptus and sea
sliding you into enchanted sleep

xxvi

Tonight's cloud—naranja, persimmon
and cinnabar—twirls like a dancer
of flamenco in a floor length dress
the beat of the sunset meeting black.

She is a fiery one, this cloud
twisting, clapping, stamping and turning
on an axis at the edge of light
knowing that soon the music will end.

In the cooling silence that follows
she will sweep you into arms and breast
the cadence of her slowing heart sweet
to your ear—tracing your path to sleep.

xxvii

Your day was spent walking on sand
leaning against a driftwood log
painting sky and sea, facing North
and smelling carne asada
cooking on a tiny grill
which we ate, charred into leather
as the sun dropped behind us
Santo and Johnny's guitars
playing Sleepwalk in your dreams.

xxviii

Tonight you stand above the clouds
looking out on new horizons
vistas of your own making.
A kind cloud rises to meet you
cradling you tenderly
as you step quiet from the cliff.

xxix

In a valley above the rain forest
mist gathers and rises in the deep night
till it hangs higher than the bounding hills
becoming playful with the dawn light.

This new-made cloud ventures forth, seeking friends.
Before long it encounters other clouds
and travels with them in the slipstream
the schoolteacher-wind showing them the world.

"All this motion and education
have nothing to do with finding a friend,"
says the cloud as he reflects on his day.
"Perhaps I need to float closer to earth?"

Dropping below the great wind, the cloud spies
a barefoot woman walking on the beach.

xxx

On nights we cannot speak
I conjure you a cloud
of contour so perfect
the angels dance and rime

their song resonating
with the rim of the earth
a gentle vibration
that leads your cloud to you

wherever you may be.

xxxi

Tonight's cloud is your cloud for every night.
It will greet you with love for all your days
holding you gently in unguarded sleep

 creating a cote safe enough to dream
in the fullness of your unbridled heart
a cloud floating between earth and heaven

in the realm where imagination leads
and the fears and scars that limit us
evaporate like dew from morning leaf.

Tonight's cloud is the cloud you have made
the cloud in need of no other
the cloud drawn from the light you have bestowed.

About the Author

Marc Zegans crafts bespoke clouds for a select clientele.
He moonlights as a poet.

www.ingramcontent.com/pod-product-compliance
Lightning Source LLC
Chambersburg PA
CBHW030419100426
42812CB00028B/3031/J